P9-AFX-318

HIP-HOP & R&B

Culture, Music & Storytelling

HIP-HOP & R&B

Culture, Music & Storytelling

Beyoncé

Bruno Mars

Cardi B

Chance the Rapper

DJ Khaled

Drake

Jay-Z

Pharrell

Pitbull

Rihanna

The Weeknd

HIP-HOP & R&B

Summer Bookout *Pitbull*

Culture, Music & Storytelling

Mason Crest
450 Parkway Drive, Suite D
Broomall, Pennsylvania 19008
(866) MCP-BOOK (toll free)

First printing
9 8 7 6 5 4 3 2 1

hardback: 978-1-4222-4184-4
series: 978-1-4222-4176-9
ebook: 978-1-4222-7626-6s

Library of Congress Cataloging-in-Publication Data

Names: Bookout, Summer, author.
Title: Pitbull / Summer Bookout.
Description: Broomall, PA : Mason Crest, 2018. | Series: Hip-hop & R&B: culture, music & storytelling.
Identifiers: LCCN 2018020774 (print) | LCCN 2018020985 (ebook) | ISBN 9781422276266 (eBook) | ISBN 9781422241844 (hardback) | ISBN 9781422241769 (series)
Subjects: LCSH: Pitbull (Rapper)--Juvenile literature. | Rap musicians--United States--Biography--Juvenile literature.
Classification: LCC ML3930.P48 (ebook) | LCC ML3930.P48 B66 2018 (print) | DDC 782.421649092 [B] --dc23
LC record available at https://lccn.loc.gov/2018020774

Developed and Produced by National Highlights, Inc.
Editor: Susan Uttendorfsky
Interior and cover design: Annalisa Gumbrecht, Studio Gumbrecht
Production: Michelle Luke

QR CODES AND LINKS TO THIRD-PARTY CONTENT

CONTENTS

Chapter 1: From Miami to the World—Pitbull's Greatest Moments 7

Chapter 2: Pitbull's Road to the Top... 21

Chapter 3: Mr. Worldwide's Growing Influence in Music and Business 31

Chapter 4: Building a Career and a Brand 51

Chapter 5: Pitbull Delivers a SLAM Dunk in Giving Back to His Community 61

Series Glossary of Key Terms 72

Further Reading 74

Internet Resources 74

Educational Videos 74

Citations... 75

Photo Credits 76

Index 77

Author's Biography 80

KEY ICONS TO LOOK FOR:

Words to understand: These words with their easy-to-understand definitions will increase the reader's understanding of the text while building vocabulary skills.

Sidebars: This boxed material within the main text allows readers to build knowledge, gain insights, explore possibilities, and broaden their perspectives by weaving together additional information to provide realistic and holistic perspectives.

Educational videos: Readers can view videos by scanning our QR codes, providing them with additional educational content to supplement the text. Examples include news coverage, moments in history, speeches, iconic sports moments, and much more!

Text-dependent questions: These questions send the reader back to the text for more careful attention to the evidence presented there.

Research projects: Readers are pointed toward areas of further inquiry connected to each chapter. Suggestions are provided for projects that encourage deeper research and analysis.

Series of glossary of key terms: This back-of-the-book glossary contains terminology used throughout this series. Words found here increase the reader's ability to read and comprehend higher-level books and articles in this field.

Chapter 1

From Miami to the World—Pitbull's Greatest Moments

A rmando Pérez chose the stage name Pitbull because of the never-give-up attitude of the pit bull dog breed. It is this same attitude that prompted the rapper to start his music career on mixtapes in Miami. Luther Campbell, a record label owner, rapper, producer, and promoter, received one of Pitbull's mixtapes from one of his talent scouts. Campbell, a member of the rap group 2LiveCrew whose music is known as "Southern Rap," was looking for a Cuban-American rapper. In the Miami area in 2001, the Latino population was a growing audience.

Pitbull's mixtape prompted Campbell to sign him as an artist with Luke Records. The young rapper accompanied him on tours, where Pitbull battled other rappers onstage in freestyle rap. That kind of rapping consists of lyrics made up on the spot, without any rehearsal.

Campbell says he begged WPOW-FM 96.5 to play Pitbull's early tracks. Now that Pitbull has international fame, Campbell says, "It's great to see a kid from the streets of Miami become a world icon."

Diaz Brothers Management and Lil Jon: The Beginning of the Road to Fame

Pitbull's appearance on Luther Campbell's single, *Lollipop*, brought him to the attention of the Diaz Brothers Management team. Lu and Hugo Diaz own a production company based in Miami and met Pitbull during a recording session for Luke Records. The Diaz brothers are well known for starting this artist on his road to fame. They are also responsible for introducing him to the famous rapper Lil Jon, who put crunk-style music into the mainstream.

Lil Jon told the *Miami New Times* that he and Pitbull met before either one of them became

Lil Jon at the 2011 American Music Awards at the Nokia Theatre L.A. Live in downtown Los Angeles. November 20, 2011, Los Angeles, CA

famous. Now they are good friends who can call each other anytime, and they have avoided any arguments in their friendship by staying close, even as their careers grew. Pitbull's freestyle rap on Lil Jon's 2002 KINGS OF KRUNK album launched him into the spotlight.

Debut Album

Pitbull's single *Oye* appeared in the movie in the 2003 movie, *2 Fast 2 Furious*. Pitbull's first full-length recording, M.I.A.M.I. (MONEY IS A MAGOR ISSUE), debuted August 24, 2004. It included the lead single *Cujo*, produced by Lil Jon, and the album sold over 655,000 copies. It reached number fourteen on the *Billboard* Top 200 and number two on the U.S. Rap Chart. That *Billboard* chart began ranking albums in 2004.

In a 2009 interview with *Miami New Times*, Lil Jon said, "I always believed in this guy [Pitbull] and I always knew he could make it commercially." Pitbull's fame and success has continued to grow from there, as he produced an album almost every year from 2005–2014. Between 2011 and 2016, many of Pitbull's singles and albums were nominated for awards in a variety of categories. He has won accolades from *Billboard* Music Awards, *Billboard* Latin Music Awards, BMI Awards (Broadcast Music, Inc.), a Grammy, and a Latin Grammy, among others.

Watch the lead single, *Cujo*, from M.I.A.M.I. (MONEY IS A MAJOR ISSUE)

Origins of Crunk—This unique type of hip-hop music differs from other styles in that it has a high-energy and club-driven feel. Instead of conversational vocals, crunk usually features hoarse chants and repeated simple choruses, with the lyrics based on the rhythm. They are perfect for playing at dance clubs.

Pitbull's music is known for club music beats, so crunk was the perfect way for him to break into the mainstream of music played on popular radio stations, not just in clubs. Four bars of music are typically created with looped electric drum machine rhythms and synthesizers that repeat throughout the song. The style first originated in the early 1990s, but did not rank on the *Billboard* Charts until the early 2000s. In 2003, the single *Get Low*—by Lil Jon and the Eastside Boyz, featuring the Ying Yang Twins—reached number two on the *Billboard* Hot 100 singles chart. By 2004, crunk was so popular that R&B star Usher asked Lil Jon to produce the single *Yeah*, which was the biggest hit of that year.

Pitbull Album Timeline

M.I.A.M.I. (MONEY IS A MAJOR ISSUE)
(Released August 03, 2004)

Pitbull's debut album combined a slight Latin flavor with "Dirty South" rap. This type of rap was first brought to the average radio listener by Luther Campbell and other Southern rap artists—like Lil Jon, Trick Daddy, and OutKast—who produced mixtapes because record labels were reluctant to sign them.

MONEY IS STILL A MAJOR ISSUE
(Released November 15, 2005)

This remix of the original 2004 album, M.I.A.M.I. (MONEY IS STILL A MAJOR ISSUE) also contains a compilation of Pitbull's best collaborations with artists like the Ying Yang Twins and Elephant Man. The release reached its highest *Billboard* rating at twenty-five, and was number two on the U.S. Rap Chart on April 15, 2006.

EL MARIEL
(Released October 30, 2006)

Featuring the single *Bojangles*, Pitbull wanted his second original album to stir more social awareness among his listeners. He noticed that his bilingual lyrics often motivated them to look up the meanings of the words, so he included more tracks about his Cuban heritage and the

Pitbull sings his first hit single, *Bojangles*

Watch *Go Girl* on YouTube

struggles of the Cuban people living in his home state of Florida. He dedicated the album to his father, José Antonio Armando Pérez Torres, who died in 2006 after a yearlong battle with cancer.

The title of the album refers to a mass emigration of Cubans into the United States from the Mariel boatlift during the 1980s. EL MARIEL topped out on the *Billboard* 200 at number seventeen and number two on the U.S. Rap Chart, while sales have exceeded 214,000.

BOATLIFT
(Released November 27, 2007)

The recording was promoted as a Spanish album, but actually, most of the songs are in English. The single *Go Girl* was featured in this album. This album only made it as high as number fifty on the *Billboard* 200, but went as high as number five on the U.S. Rap Chart.

PITBULL STARRING IN REBELUTION
(Released August 28, 2009)

This album, full of "slick club cuts," produced three major hit singles, including *I Know You Want Me (Calle Ocho)*, an international hit that peaked at number two on the *Billboard* Hot 100 Chart. More than 1.6 million digital copies of *I Know You Want Me (Calle Ocho)* were sold and in 2009, the video for the song became the most watched music video on YouTube. The single won Best

Latin Song on the MP3 Music Awards, which are open to any artist who is eighteen years or older. Musicians simply fill out the form and download their song for consideration and the winners are chosen by popular vote.

The single *Bon, Bon* won Top Latin Song at the *Billboard* Music Awards in 2011 and 2012. REBELUTION reached number eight on the *Billboard* 200 Chart and has sold over 174,000 copies.

I Know You Want Me was the second single released off the REBELUTION album. The reference to Calle Ocho is a street in the Little Havana neighborhood where Pitbull lived as a child.

ARMONDO
(Released November 02, 2010)

Pitbull's first all-Spanish-language album only made it to number sixty-five on the *Billboard* 200 Chart, but rose to second on the U.S. Rap Chart. The album was named after Pitbull's father, who went by the name Armando. It won the Lo Nuestro Award for Urban Album of the Year. This award, presented by presented by Univision, a U.S. Spanish-language television network, recognizes the most talented performers of Latin music.

Popular restaurant in Little Havana neighborhood

PLANET PIT
(Released June 17, 2011)

Two major hit singles, *Hey Baby (Drop It to The Floor)* and *Give Me Everything*, exploded off this album. In 2012, *Give Me Everything* won Top Radio Song at the *Billboard* Music Awards and Song of the Year on the *Billboard* Latin Music Awards. PLANET PIT reached number seven on the *Billboard* 200 Chart and number two on the U.S. Rap Chart, with over 50,000 copies having been sold.

GLOBAL WARMING
(November, 06 2012)

Back in Time, the lead single from GLOBAL WARMING, was featured in the movie *Men in Black 3*—the first time someone other than Will Smith sang a *Men in Black* theme song. On the *Billboard* 200 Chart, GLOBAL WARMING's highest ranking was fourteen, but it reached the top of the rap chart. Over 355,000 copies have been sold so far.

GLOBAL WARMING: MELTDOWN
(Released November 22, 2013)

This album was released as an extended play version of the songs on GLOBAL WARMING, but there were also five bonus tracks and many guest artists, such as Shakira, Jennifer Lopez, and Afrojack.

Watch Pitbull and T-Pain sing this explosive hit, *Hey Baby (Drop It to The Floor)* from PLANET PIT

GLOBALIZATION
(Released November 21, 2014)

Pitbull's eighth studio album reached number eighteen on the *Billboard* chart and number three on the U.S. Rap Chart, with more than 198,000 copies sold. Four singles from this extremely successful album reached the *Billboard* Top 40: *Wild Wild Love, Fireball, Time of Our Lives,* and *Fun*.

DALE
(Released July 07, 2015)

The title means "hit it" in Spanish. This album reached number ninety-seven on the *Billboard* 200 Chart and number three on the U.S. Rap Chart. Pitbull won his first Grammy Award—Best Latin Rock Urban or Alternative Album—for this recording in February of 2016.

CLIMATE CHANGE
(Released March 17, 2016)

Robin Thicke, Enrique Iglesias, and R. Kelly—among others—collaborated on different singles with Pitbull for this album. His duet with Jennifer Lopez, *Sexy Body*, is one of the featured singles. CLIMATE CHANGE climbed to number twenty-nine on the *Billboard* 200 Chart and number twelve on the U.S. Rap Chart.

Robin Thicke

Tours

Along with recording albums, Pitbull has also performed live many times and has participated in several concert tours.

The Rebelution Tour

Pitbull's first world tour lasted from 2009 to 2011 and included over thirty stops in the United States. A total of fifty-five shows were scheduled as he traveled between the United States, Europe, South America, Africa, Mexico, Canada, and Asia. Pitbull told *Billboard's* Mariel Concepcion,

"Rebelution stands for fighter, I feel like I've been fighting in music and creating new opportunities to make things work even when people thought it wouldn't."

He also explained that the name of the album and tour is a combination of the words *revolution* and *rebel*. The rapper stated, "The word 'revolution' is a strong word, and the word 'rebel' is powerful. Because you're looking for a change, that's what revolution is, but when you're a fighter in it, you're fighting for that change."

The Planet Pit Tour

Pitbull's second world tour began with performances in South America. The tour ran from January 13 to November 02, of 2012 with additional stops in North America, Europe, Asia,

Pitbull singing his Top Latin Song, *Bon, Bon*

Back in Time, the lead single from Global Warming and *Men in Black 3* theme song and Australia. A total of eighty-one shows were scheduled to be completed within 293 days. Promotions for the tour led to packed venues in San Francisco in the United States and five different big cities in Australia, with 80–100 percent of seats sold. Fellow Florida rapper, Flo Rida, opened the concert in Canada.

The North American Tour

Ke$ha joined Pitbull on this tour that promoted Pitbull's GLOBAL WARMING and Ke$ha's WARRIOR. E! Network filmed the June 07, 2013, concert and broadcast it on June 21 as the first show of the E!'s Inside Track Summer Concert Series.

Before the tour, Pitbull and Ke$ha got their fans' attention by tweeting about it. The duo traveled to shows from Boston, Massachusetts, to Tampa, Florida. An Australian leg was scheduled, but shows at the five venues were canceled due to low ticket sales.

Enrique Iglesias and Pitbull Live

The 2017 tour has audiences up out of their seats at every show. According to *Billboard*, Enrique Iglesias's part of the concert is full of surprises and love for his fans, while Pitbull's portion, of course, features all the songs people want to dance to.

The tour, with thirty-five scheduled shows, kicked off on June 03, 2017, in Chicago's Allstate Arena with a sold-out concert. BillboardBiz.com reports that the first fourteen concerts have been sellouts, so the tour's success continues! The circuit is expected to end in October 2017, after stops in many American and Canadian cities.

Watch the *Billboard* Top 40 video for *Fireball*

Jennifer Lopez

Watch Pitbull's duet
with Jennifer Lopez

Words to Understand

expatriate: to withdraw (oneself) from residence in one's country.

influx: the act of flowing in.

dictator: a ruler who has absolute power and unrestricted control over a government.

anti-imperialism: against the authority of one nation over another foreign country.

socialism: government-controlled wealth that is distributed to the people of the country.

Chapter 2

Pitbull's Road to the Top

The Beginning of the Journey to the Top

Armando Christian Pérez's road to the top of the entertainment business was not a smooth one. Even his stage name, Pitbull, reflects how he has worked hard and struggled to attain the fame and fortune he now enjoys.

He was born January 15, 1981, to Alysha Acosta and José Antonio Armando Pérez Torres. His parents were **expatriates** from Cuba who came to Miami to escape Fidel Castro's dictatorship. Alysha and José Antonio (usually called Armando) separated before Pitbull was four years old, and from that time on, he was raised primarily by his mother.

She and Pitbull moved all over Miami when he was young, living in some of the city's roughest neighborhoods. The city experienced an **influx** of Cuban refugees the year before Pitbull was born, when one 150,000 people emigrated as part of the Mariel boatlift initiated by the Cuban **dictator**, Castro.

Fidel Castro—Fidel Castro was born in 1926 into a wealthy family, with his father owning a sugar plantation. Castro was considered intellectually gifted at an early age. As a college student, he studied law at the University of Havana. There he became interested in Cuban nationalism, **anti-imperialism**, and **socialism**, joining a group called "The Movement" to oppose Batista, the country's dictator at that time. The group led a strike on a military barracks. The attack failed and resulted in Castro and his brother Raul being put in prison in 1953.

Castro continued coordinating his resistance movement while he was in jail, while he was out of the country, and from inside the country. By the age of thirty-two, in February 1959, he had taken control and was sworn in as Cuba's prime minister.

Castro repeatedly denied being a communist leader, but signed agreements to buy oil from the Soviet Union, resulting in a strain on Cuba's relationship with the United States. President Eisenhower broke diplomatic ties with Cuba before 1961, and the United States banned all trading with the country in 1962.

Hundreds of thousands of Cubans fled to Florida because of the lack of human rights under Castro's control. Many of the country's people were executed for speaking out against Castro and his government.

South Florida—and especially Miami—in the early 1980s was considered to be unstable by most people. More and more people were buying, selling, and using drugs, and the crime rates rose. Unfortunately, Pitbull's father drank too much alcohol and got caught up in the flourishing drug trade of Miami during the 1980s.

A boat crowded with Cuban refugees arrives in Key West, FL, during the 1980 Mariel boatlift

But Armando took the time to teach his son the power of words by having him memorize the poetry of José Martí. As young as three years old, Pitbull recited poetry for patrons in the bars where his father hung out.

Cuban Cultural Influences in Miami

The Miami that Pitbull grew up in was full of Cuban emigrants. Some had lived in Miami for years, like his parents, but others were part of a more recent wave of newcomers in the 1990s. Each brought their culture with them from the island.

Cuban cultural influences have continued to affect Miami, and by 2010, 35 percent of Miami's population was Cuban. Forty percent of the population were people whose dominant language was Spanish. The neighborhood area west of downtown Miami is known as Little

Miami, FL – December 18, 2016: Colorful artwork and signage on display at the entrance to the popular Calle Ocho in historic Little Havana

Havana, and it was established by the 500,000 Cubans who moved there in the 1960s.

The neighborhood acquired its name from the largest city in Cuba and its capital, Havana. It spans 8th Street—*Calle Ocho* in Spanish. Pitbull's songs often reference "Calle Ocho" because of the time he spent living in Little Havana as a child.

Role Models

By the time he was in high school, Pitbull had started rapping. The rapper Nas was a major influence, as was West Coast rap and the Miami bass genre of hip-hop. Pitbull briefly attended South Miami Senior High

View of 8th Street in Little Havana, a focal point of the Cuban community in Miami

School, which boasts of having the Celia Cruz Magnet Program with the Celia Cruz School of the Arts. While Pitbull later cited Celia Cruz as a role model and inspiration, there is little information about the time he may have spent in this magnet program.

He attended several different schools during his academic career because he and his mother moved around Miami, depending on her job at the time. Pitbull eventually graduated from Coral Park High School in 1998. Both high schools he attended were primarily Hispanic, with over half the student body claiming Hispanic heritage.

Fast Fact 3:

Celia Cruz—This famous Cuban singer is known for her powerful voice and rhythm-centered musical style. She was the most popular Latin artist of the twentieth century, with twenty-three certified Gold albums in her career, spanning from the early 1940s until the early 2000s. In 1994, President Bill Clinton awarded the National Medal of Arts to the internationally known "Queen of Salsa." Around the same time, *Billboard* reporter Leila Cobo described her as "…the best known and influential female figure in the history of Cuban Latin music."

Pitbull's Early Years

When Pitbull was young, he did not necessarily take advantage of his educational opportunities. He says he was given his high school diploma simply so the principal would not have to see him for another year. And during his high school years, Pitbull's mother discovered the seventeen-year-old was following in his father's

footsteps by selling drugs. She kicked him out of the house, and thereafter, he was on his own in some of the roughest Miami neighborhoods. He also spent time with a foster family in Roswell, Georgia.

Pitbull does not share many details of that time in his life. However, he continued to rap and decided to leave the illegal and dangerous drug-trade lifestyle behind in favor of furthering his music career. Pitbull admits that Armando was an alcoholic, but despite that, he gave the young rapper a strong drive to succeed. His parents lived together again for a short period after his father's house burned down. It was then that Pitbull realized who he was and what he wanted.

His dream became reality in 2004 with the release of his debut album, M.I.A.M.I. (Money is a Major Issue). The album hit number thirty-two on the *Billboard* Hot 100 Chart and number eleven on the Hot Rap Tracks Chart—released weekly by *Billboard* and listing the top twenty-five most popular hip-hop songs. The songs are ranked based on radio airplay and sales for the week.

Importance of Education

Although he did not pursue a college education, Pitbull was awarded an honorary degree from a private non-profit institution in 2014—Florida's Doral College. Anitere Flores, President of the college, believes Pitbull deserved the unspecified honorary degree because of his

 Tireless devotion to his community and improving educational access.

Pitbull wants better schools to be made available for the kids in the neighborhoods he grew up in, because he feels his own educational experience was lacking. Education is also important to the superstar because he has six children of his own, ranging from elementary school age to high school age. He

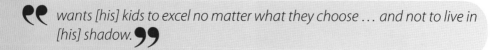 *wants [his] kids to excel no matter what they choose … and not to live in [his] shadow.*

Two of his children, Destiny and Bryce Pérez, were born to Spanish model Barbara Alba. As a careful and conscientious father, Pitbull keeps his younger children out of the spotlight as much as possible. He doesn't want them to feel they have to follow in his footsteps, and wants them to be whoever they are.

Text-Dependent Questions:

❶ Where is Calle Ocho, and why is it important to Pitbull?

❷ How many children does Pitbull have with Barbara Alba?

❸ What college gave Pitbull an honorary degree?

Research Project:

❶ Find out more about life in Cuba today. Who runs the government? What is their education system like? What jobs do people have?

Words to Understand

endorsement: money earned from a product recommendation, typically by a celebrity, athlete, or other public figure.

ally: v. to connect through a relationship, to support; n. a person, group, or nation that is associated with another or others for some common cause or purpose.

demographic: a specific part of the population having shared characteristics.

equity: the value of a business in terms of money.

innovative: introducing or creating something new or different.

Chapter 3

Mr. Worldwide's Growing Influence in Music and Business

Pitbull is Recognized for His Talent

Pitbull's hard work and dedication to his music finally began to pay off as his fan base grew. Luther Campbell had first recruited Pitbull because his Cuban heritage would appeal to the growing Latino population in the United States. Pitbull's music is enjoyed by listeners from all ethnic and economic backgrounds. Because of this, he has achieved success on Latin and non-Latin charts.

Enrique Iglesias performing with Pitbull at the Frank Erwin Center in Austin, TX, 2015

AWARDS

American Music Awards

Favorite Artist, Latin Music | Nominated in 2012

Favorite Male Artist,
Pop or Rock Music | Nominated in 2012

American Latino Media Arts Award

Favorite Male Music Artist | Won in 2011 and 2012

Billboard Latin Music Awards

Latin Digital Download Artist of the Year |
Won in 2009

Hot Latin Song of the Year, Vocal Event Award—
I Like It, featuring Enrique Iglesias | Won in 2011

Songs Artist of the Year, Male Award | Won in 2012

Latin Rhythm Song, Solo Artist
of the Year | Won in 2012

Song of the Year—*Give Me Everything* | Won in 2012

Broadcast Music Inc. Awards (BMI)

Latin Songwriter of the Year—*I Like It*, co-written with Enrique Iglesias | Won in 2012

Latin Award Winning Song—*I Like It*, co-written with Enrique Iglesias | Won in 2012

President's Award—For his influence in the entertainment industry | Won in 2012

Grammy Awards

Best Latin Rock Urban or Alternative Album— Dale | Won in 2016

Latin Grammy Awards

Best Urban Performance— *Echa Pálla* and *Manos Párriba* | Won in 2013

Premio Lo Nuestro

Urban and General Artist of the Year | Won in 2011
Favorite Hip-Hop Artist | Won in 2012
Best Album of the Year—Armando | Won in 2012

Billboard Music Awards

Top Rap Artist | Won in 2014
Top Rap Song—*Timber*, featuring Ke$ha | Won in 2014

Hollywood Walk of Fame

Pitbull's star on the Hollywood Walk of Fame was unveiled on July 15, 2016. It was the 2,584th star to be awarded and was given in the recording category. Pitbull's financial mentor, Tony Robbins, and music legend Luther Campbell were speakers at the unveiling ceremony. Ana Martinez, producer of the Walk of Fame Ceremonies, summed up the reason for awarding Pitbull the star. "The world is fascinated by Pitbull's story and his remarkable talent. The Hollywood community welcomes him with open arms and applauds him for his work by placing him on one of the world's most famous landmarks, the Hollywood Walk of Fame."

Pitbull's star on the Hollywood Walk of Fame is within a few steps of his idol, Celia Cruz. The estate of Celia Cruz presented Pitbull with one of her beautiful shoes showcased in a Lucite box during the unveiling ceremony of his star.

Pitbull Is Not Afraid to Work for His Success

Armando Pérez reminds people why he chose the stage name Pitbull—because those dogs do not give up. He did not give up just because he had to work to accomplish his fame and has grown in music and business from Mr. 305—referring to Miami's telephone area code—to Mr. Worldwide. He not only sells albums and travels the world but he has global business interests as well.

Pitbull is known as a celebrity who actively seeks product and brand **endorsements** and is widely pursued by a range of

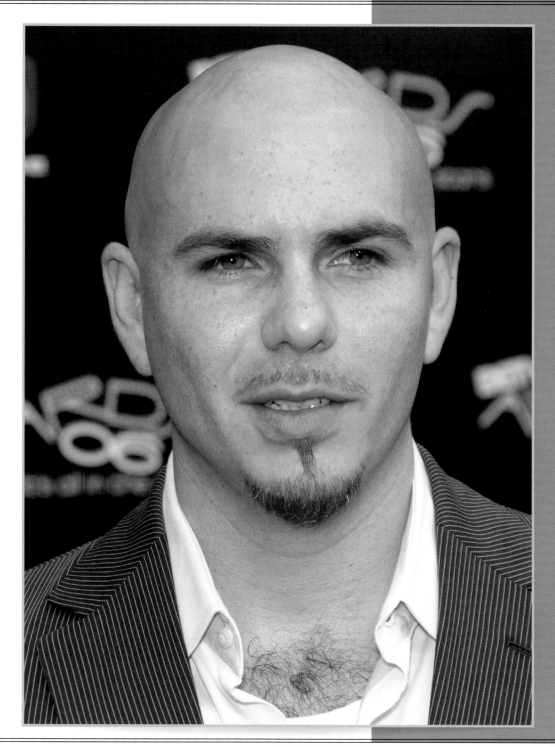

businesses, from soft drinks to cruise lines. He told CNBC, "I love the hustle, I love the grind, and I love the fight." He is a self-proclaimed workaholic who says he only needs four hours of sleep a night. That leaves plenty of time to not only write music, but build a business empire as well.

Endorsements

Corporate America has come to recognize the growing Latino market and the buying power it has. This makes companies like Dr. Pepper, Pepsi, Kodak, Fiat Chrysler Automobiles, and even Walmart clamor to have Mr. Worldwide endorse their products. Pitbull's social media presence alone makes him a huge business **ally**. His Twitter connections number 2.2 million, while on Instagram, the number increases to 2.5 million. But the number of Facebook followers far outnumbers both, at 59 million.

Every time Pitbull tweets, posts a picture, or writes a status update, he has the power to reach tens of millions of people instantly. Businesses want to tap into his influence through product endorsements.

Kodak

This American company did just that when they picked Drake, Trey Songz, Pitbull, and Rihanna to endorse the Kodak M590 EasyShare digital camera. The camera features a Share button that allows users to instantly tag pictures for email or for Facebook, Twitter, Flickr, and Kodak Gallery. This plays to Pitbull's social media influence, as well as his music influence.

Dr. Pepper

Dr. Pepper proved Pitbull's influence over the Latino population when his endorsement upped their sales by 1.7 percent in that **demographic** alone.

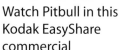

Watch Pitbull in this Kodak EasyShare commercial

Dr. Pepper commercial featuring Pitbull

Norwegian Cruise Line

Norwegian Cruise Line bills Pitbull as the "Godfather of [their] ship, *Norwegian Escape*." The ad campaign claims, "Pitbull wants you to feel free to take the party worldwide." The commercial features his single, *Freedom*, and he was present to christen the ship as well. The ad campaign began in 2016 and is ongoing. A cruise titled "Pitbull's After-Dark Party" on the *Norwegian Pearl* set sail in the fall of 2017. This cruise left from Pitbull's beloved Miami and sailed to the Bahamas. Passengers were treated to live performances by Pitbull during their time on the ship.

Fiat Chrysler Automobiles

This company, founded in 1900, chose Pitbull for their multi-cultural Dodge Dart ad campaign targeting millennials. The Spanish/English advertisements were produced through a Houston and Los Angeles–based Hispanic agency. Pitbull's Clear Channel Media and Entertainment Tour were sponsored by Dodge. The tour consisted of eleven events that led up to the 2012 iHeartMusic Festival in Las Vegas. Everyone who took a Dodge Dart for a test drive was entered into the sweepstakes for two tickets to the festival. They also had the chance to meet

Pitbull backstage and win a 2013 Dodge Dart. The lucky winner, from New York, was personally handed the keys by the rapper.

Pitbull wrote the music for the radio and television commercials and called out his famous catchphrase, *"Dale!"* ("Go ahead!") during the ads. Dodge chose Pitbull because he is "hip, **innovative**, and relevant to millennials, yet has crossover appeal as well." The millennial age group includes people born from those born from the late 1980s to the early 2000s. The Dart is a popular car among them and so is Pitbull!

The Dodge Dart at the 2013 Chicago Auto Show on February 07, 2013

Watch Pitbull's Dodge
Dart commercial

How Companies Encourage You to Buy Their Products

Businesses big and small spend a lot of money to advertise products like water, soft drinks, cars, clothes, perfume, and food. These companies want people to purchase their merchandise, so they use certain kinds of advertising techniques to draw people in. They want you to see their product as better so you will buy theirs rather than the same, or a similar, product from their competition.

The techniques below are just some of the ways companies get us to buy their products.

➔ **Bandwagon:** This kind of marketing campaign urges people to buy the products because "everyone else is." The merchandise must be good because so many other consumers are buying it.

➔ **Celebrity Spokesperson/Hero Worship:** Pitbull is famous for these types of endorsements. When he appears in an advertisement for a company, people transfer their respect and admiration for him to the product. He influences his fans to buy a car, drink, etc. because he likes it too, so it's similar to a bandwagon marketing promotion, only with a celebrity.

➔ **Emotional Appeals:** These commercials make viewers feel certain emotions, like excitement. The positive reaction transfers to the product and encourages them to buy it. Any commercial starring Pitbull in his famous party atmosphere would have great emotional appeal to his fans.

→ **Glittering Generalities:** These ads emphasize highly valued and strongly held beliefs like patriotism, peace, or freedom. Pitbull's advertisement for Norwegian Cruise Line uses this type of marketing technique as well. The name of his single associated with the cruise line is *Freedom*, and the commercial offers customers the feeling of being free if they reserve a trip on one of its boats.

→ **Individuality:** This type of advertisement appeals to consumers' desires to be different from everyone else, which is the opposite of the bandwagon. People are encouraged to celebrate their own style or rebel against what others are doing by purchasing this product because it looks and feels unique, stylish, or cool. Pitbull's SiriusXM radio station is an example of this. More details later!

Pitbull and Miami Subs Grill

Pitbull often searches for companies to endorse in return for **equity** in that company. Not only is he a smart businessperson, but he's determined to plan for his children's financial stability and give back to the community when he can.

This is exactly how he came to be involved with Miami Subs Grill, his favorite Miami restaurant chain when he was growing up. A trip there was a treat, and he has always liked Miami Subs Grill's chicken wings and gyro platter. The Miami Beach restaurant on Washington Avenue served as his second office, where he went to write songs. Pitbull even joked with the owner about buying the restaurant someday.

In 2012, Mr. 305 purchased significant equity in Miami Subs Grill. He is determined to help revive the chain that boomed in Miami during the 1980s and early 1990s by investing in it and rebranding it The Miami Grill. The exact terms of the deal were not released, but Pitbull has expansion rights into some parts of Latin America and the Caribbean.

He stated,

> *What's better than Mr. 305 to be involved with Miami Subs? It's about two Miami brands being able to grow together. Where we can take it is limitless.*

Pitbull's Other Business Interests

In a 2013 interview with Cecilia Vega and ABC News, Pitbull answered her question of his net worth by saying, "Even if you wanted to count it, you couldn't." However, in 2016, at age thirty-five he's worth an estimated $65 million…or more. Investing in shrewd business ventures—like owning his own SiriusXM radio station and a television development company, and releasing fragrance lines—have increased his popularity, influence, and net worth.

SiriusXM Radio Station

Pitbull's *Globalization Worldwide Rhythmic Hits* SiriusXM station was launched with a live show from New York City's Apollo Theater on May 19, 2015. The channel plays hits from around the world and the concept was influenced by Pitbull's musical influence and his love of international acts.

The Apollo Theater is a landmark in Harlem

Named after Pitbull's 2014 album, GLOBALIZATION, the commercial-free station offers listeners music he's created with other artists, live performances, and exclusive mix shows. Other musical influences in Pitbull's life—from Celia Cruz to Nas—are also played.

Pitbull and Endemol Shine North America

In 2014, Pitbull and Endemol Shine North America signed a deal to develop and produce original content for digital platforms. Pitbull announced his plans to work with the production company onstage at their 2014 party during the National Association of Television Program Executives (NATPE) in Miami Beach. Pitbull will be involved in television development as well as digital offshoots. There are hopes of producing a Pitbull YouTube Channel through the new EndemolShine Beyond digital unit of the company. Endemol hopes to create a premium network of international and local channels across platforms like YouTube, Yahoo!, and AOL.

In a 2014 interview with Variety.com, Cris Abrego, the CEO of Endemol, stated, "Combining Pitbull's already massive global presence with our Endemol Beyond digital dream team and our creative scripted and unscripted teams in a first of its kind deal will give us an opportunity to create groundbreaking content across all media."

Pitbull's Fragrance Lines

Scents for both men and women were first released in 2013 with the name Pitbull. In August 2015, Mr. Worldwide released follow-up fragrances, one for men and one for women, named Pitbull Miami. He wanted the scent—reminiscent of Miami's summer days, South Beach, balmy nights, and, of course, club beats—to be a bottled reminder of his hometown. Pitbull says he started layering scents he liked until he found the right combination. The women's scents are sweet, while the men's versions are richer, musky scents.

Commercial Realm

While the international superstar is busy building an empire of investments and commercial ventures, he told CNBC,

> ❝ *The music business is 90 percent business, 10 percent talent. It's great that you can rap. It's great that you can sing … but if you don't understand the business, then the people around you are going to take advantage of your business.* ❞

In order to understand commercial and financial operations even better, Pitbull has turned to people outside the music industry—like Warren Buffett, Carlos Slim, and Tony Robbins—to be his mentors.

Tony Robbins—Best-Selling Author, Motivational Speaker, and Entrepreneur

Alysha, Armando Pérez's mother, played Tony Robbins' Personal Power inspirational cassette tapes in the car on the way to drop him off at school. Robbins's stories made an impression on the young man long before he became Pitbull. His

Tony Robbins & wife arrives at CNN's Larry King Live final broadcast party at Spago on December 16, 2010, in Beverly HIlls, CA

mother's insistence that he listen to Robbins's motivational lessons helped him to see the word "no" as a challenge. In his career, as he told CNBC, he wants people to tell him a new project is not as good as a previous project. Then he is motivated to make the new project or album even better.

Watch Pitbull's CNBC interview about the naysayers

Fast Fact 4:

Who is Warren Buffett?—Born in Omaha, Nebraska, on August 30, 1930, Warren Buffett is now near the top of the *Forbes* list of world billionaires on a yearly basis. As a young boy, he showed great abilities in mathematics, often helping in his father's stockbrokerage office. At the age of eleven, he made his first stock investment. He sold it for a small profit but learned investment patience when the stock price rose dramatically after he sold his shares.

Warren Buffett, the Chairman of Berkshire Hathaway, in the Oval Office, July 18, 2011

By age thirteen, Buffett was running his own business as a paperboy and selling his own horse-racing tip sheet. When his father was elected to the U.S. House of Representatives, his family moved to Virginia. He and a high school friend bought a pinball machine and put it in a barber shop. Within a few months, they had made enough to buy more machines. He sold the business for $1,200. He entered college at age sixteen and by the time he graduated at age twenty, he had made $10,000 from his various businesses.

After graduating from Columbia Business School with a master's degree, Buffett worked in finance. In 1956, he went back to Omaha and became a millionaire through his financial investments. He started by buying stock in a textile company, Berkshire Hathaway. He then expanded Berkshire Hathaway by phasing out

textiles and investing in media. He financed companies like *The Washington Post*, GEICO, and Exxon. He invested in Coca-Cola and was on the company's board of directors from 1989–2006.

In 2006, he announced that he was giving 85 percent of his fortune to the Bill and Melinda Gates Foundation, resulting in the largest single act of charitable giving in the United States.

Carlos Slim—Business Tycoon, Investor, and Philanthropist

Carlos Slim is a Mexican businessman who consistently ranks at the top of *Forbes*' list of the world's billionaires. The rankings are calculated by a person's net worth, and from 2010–2013, Slim was considered the richest person in the world.

Slim learned how to invest and studied accounting while working for his father's investment company. He has businesses in many industries, including education, health care, industrial manufacturing, real estate, media, technology, and sports. Pitbull admires Slim and his success in business.

Mexican billionaire business tycooon and philanthropist Carlos Slim arrives on the red carpet for the Friars Foundation gala at the Waldorf Astoria hotel in New York City on October 07, 2014

Text-Dependent Questions:

❶ Name at least two products Pitbull has endorsed.

❷ What type of marketing techniques have been used by companies in advertisements featuring Pitbull?

❸ What is played on Pitbull's SiriusXM station?

Research Project:

❶ Create a chart with five different celebrities and products they have endorsed. How much money did each celebrity make on the deal?

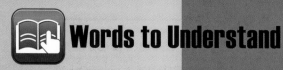

Words to Understand

choreography:
the art of planning and arranging the movements, steps, and patterns of dancers.

cardiovascular:
relating to the heart and all of the body's blood vessels.

endeavors:
in the business world, to apply yourself with effort in starting, enlarging, or sustaining a commercial activity, or to try a new concept.

collaboration:
a product created by working with someone else; combining individual talents.

Chapter 4

Building a Career and a Brand

Building a Music Career Through Collaboration

Working together with Lil Jon on singles was the beginning of Pitbull's career. He continued to **collaborate** with Lil Jon and the Eastside Boyz, and the Ying Yang Twins, as his career grew. In 2004, a partnership with Usher produced the biggest single of the year—*Yeah*.

Pitbull's 2005 album M.I.A.M.I. (MONEY IS A MAJOR ISSUE) features the best of his collaborations at the time, including *Everybody Get Up* with Pretty Ricky, which showcases Pitbull's ability to produce a crunk single. Another song on that album, *Rah Rah*, features Elephant Man and has a distinct Jamaican feel to it.

His work with Latin superstar Enrique Iglesias on the single *I Like It* (2012) defined Pitbull as the person to team up with for successful collaborations. During his career, he has become a master at partnering with new, up-and-coming artists—as well as the more well-known, established performers—to create hit after hit. *Timber* (2014), which has a country flair that his other songs do not, was a major sensation with Ke$ha. *International Love* (2011) featured Chris Brown as the vocalist.

Collaborations on Climate Change
(Released March 17, 2017)

The CLIMATE CHANGE album features teamwork on almost every single. The album was released in March 2017 and debuted at number nine on the *Billboard* 200 Chart. It includes these singles:

- *Messin' Around*, featuring Enrique Iglesias.

- *Greenlight*, featuring Flo Rida and LunchMoney Lewis.

- *Bad Man*, featuring Robin Thicke, Joe Perry, and Travis Barker, was the closing number at the 58th Annual Grammy Awards.

Pitbull has discovered the way to deliver hit after hit is to combine his talents with the skills of others, thereby bringing out the best in everyone.

Collaborations with Jennifer Lopez

One of the most notable partnerships Pitbull has arranged is teaming up with Jennifer Lopez. They first worked together in 2009 on Lopez's track *Fresh out of the Oven*. The song was a promotional single released in anticipation of her seventh album, LOVE? It debuted online in October and did well on the dance charts, abruptly shooting up to number fourteen on the U.S. Hot Dance Club Songs Chart. The song was popular in clubs, but never caught on in mainstream radio.

In 2011, Pitbull was featured on Lopez's lead single for the album LOVE? The single, titled *On the Floor*, also featured Ne-Yo, Afrojack, and Nayer.

On the Floor made its debut on *Billboard's* Hot 100 Chart at number nine and eventually topped charts in Australia, Canada, Germany, and the United Kingdom. Within six weeks after its release, more than 600,000 copies had been sold in the United States.

In 2014, Pitbull and Jennifer Lopez had the honor of recording the FIFA World Cup Anthem *We Are One (Ole Ola)* with Brazilian singer Claudia Leitte. The three artists performed the song at the opening ceremonies in Brazil on June 12, 2014.

Constructing a Brand through Commercial Ventures

Samba school parade Unidos de Padre Miguel during the 2016 carnival in Rio de Janeiro, the Sambodromo, Queen of percussion Claudia Leitte

Pitbull's belief that his music career is 90 percent business has driven him not only to endorse products, but to build his own name as a brand. Part of this brand construction began in early 2011 when he formed a partnership with Zumba® Fitness, an aerobic exercise and dance program company. The company was a partnership perfect fit with Mr. 305 because, like him, it started in Miami and is still based there.

Pitbull, Lil Jon, and other musicians teamed up with the company to release new singles geared specifically for Zumba. Beto Perez, co-founder of Zumba, believes that "Major names in music [have] recognized that it's good business to be with Zumba. These artists are talented, write catchy music, and they get people hooked."

In October 2011, Pitbull invited the global dance-fitness company to join him on the month-long Euphoria Tour with Enrique Iglesias. The Zumba dancers were onstage with him in the three tour locations: Newark, New Jersey; Los Angeles, California; and, of course, Miami. Zumba celebrities Gina Grant, Tanya Beardsley, and Beto Perez performed a customized routine for *Pause*, a single from the album PLANET PIT, during these special concert appearances.

Perez **choreographed** the moves, and the event was recorded as a video for *Pause*. The dance routine's video has received over a million views, with the steps being copied by Zumba fans all over the world. CEO of Zumba Fitness, Alberto Perlman, boasted that "Zumba is the only fitness company to ever go on tour with a major recording artist."

Pitbull also performed with Zumba Fitness dancers at the Fifth Annual American Latin Music Awards, where he won the prestigious Best Male Music Artist award. Mr. Worldwide and other musicians have expanded their fan bases through Zumba by exposing people who would not necessarily hear their music to the catchy beats and lyrics.

Zumba is marketed as a fitness party, and Pitbull knows how to create party beats and rhythms that move people to dance. Pitbull was in Orlando for the 2011 annual convention of over 6,000 licensed instructors, and performed in the Zumba Fitness Concert.

At the 2011 Zumba convention, he told *MTV News* that he sees the partnership in this light: "The way Zumba has done it is taken all those things that maybe we've all learned from different countries and put it into a form where it's global now." Like Pitbull, Zumba has a vast social media connection that furthers its worldwide reach.

Fast Fact 6:

The Zumba Fitness Trend—When Beto Perez substituted salsa and merengue for his traditional aerobics class music, he did not realize that he would start a worldwide fitness craze. Perez eventually brought the idea to Miami in 1999. By 2001, along with Alberto Perlman and Alberto Aghion, Perez had trademarked the name and began marketing the workouts as a dance party. The music featured in the workouts has roots in Latin dances, like merengue, salsa, and samba. Zumba began as a dance-fitness concept and has developed into a massive lifestyle brand.

The global programs include classes for every stage of life and level of fitness. Zumbatomics is designed for children, while Zumba Gold is a class for active older adults. These classes, along with DVDs and a video game, have allowed over 14 million people in

185 countries to participate in some type of Zumba workout. The video game plays music from over thirty global genres, including salsa, Tahitian, calypso, Bollywood, Irish step, and reggaetón (combining rap with Caribbean rhythms).

Traditional Zumba includes high-intensity **cardiovascular** exercise sessions that last fifty to sixty minutes. The raucous "fitness party" offers a total body workout that tones and sculpts muscles and burns fat while dancing to upbeat international rhythms. The Zumba brand has "defied all the odds and broken all the rules by bringing together a seemingly mismatched team … to create not only the next generation in fitness but an entirely new platform for both artist and consumer."

Watch Zumba's dance routine for *Pause*

Pitbull's New Year's Eve Special

Mr. 305 is always looking for ways to spotlight and assist his hometown of Miami. His *New Year's Revolution* television broadcast is a way for him to do both.

The special first aired on December 31, 2014, and was co-produced by Endemol Shine North America and Pitbull's own production company, Honey I'm Home. The Fox Broadcasting Company airs the special and it is scheduled to run on New Year's at least through 2017. The 2014 and 2015 specials were broken into segments, with the first part playing from eight to ten p.m., and a ninety-minute segment starting at eleven o'clock Eastern Standard Time.

For New Year's Eve 2016, the city of Miami expanded the party into a two-day festival called the "Norwegian Worldwide Food and Wine Party." Miami Mayor Tómas Pedro Regalado thought it would be great publicity for Miami to be the focus of the television special. Miami's "Big Orange" would be in direct competition with the famous ball drop in Times Square, New York.

In 2017, the special was co-hosted by Queen Latifah and Snoop Dogg. *Hollywood Reporter* stated that the Fox Broadcasting Company wanted to partner with these globally relevant pop stars to capitalize on Pitbull's reach.

The show is a success, with over 2 million viewers each year.

Pitbull's Global Music and Dance Lyrics

Pitbull's involvement with both Zumba Fitness and the New Year's Eve special are perfect examples of what he wants his music to accomplish. He stated in a *Variety* magazine interview:

> I just want to make global music, bottom line ... I love music that makes you want to get up and lose your mind and have fun ... Some people might like music that's more emotional...but I want to have very quick punchlines, something people can sing along to because I think that's what makes timeless records.

His most famous catchphrase is "*Dale!*" which roughly translates into "Go ahead!" in English. Pitbull simply wants his listeners to get up and dance. His music's beats and rhythms drive listeners' impulse to dance, and the simple, catchy lyrics get people to sing along. His lyrics may not be deeply political or emotional, but they are not meant to be. These are party songs, through and through. When speaking of politics before a concert, he said, "With everything that's going on in the world right [now], let's forget about that tonight … I don't believe in politics … I actually call them 'poli-tricks.'"

While some may criticize his cavalier approach to music, Mr. Worldwide is literally a global superstar. His lyrics and attitude may seem frivolous, but the business behind them is serious. In an interview with *Variety*, Pitbull stated, "There's no magic trick, there's no silver bullet, there's no cutting corners when it comes to building businesses. Because that's what you gotta do, you've gotta build 'em."

Big fireworks over the skyline of downtown Miami

He has not just built a business but a brand empire, with his name at the forefront of his partnerships with many different types of businesses. Through the lyrics of his songs, the commercial enterprises he partners with, and the brands he endorses, he chooses to send his message of "Just let everything go and have fun."

His dedication to his hometown of Miami is obvious in his lyrics—and in his self-appointed nickname, "Mr. 305"—but it also evident in the many business **endeavors** he has with Miami-based companies.

Text-Dependent Questions:

❶ Who created Zumba? Why is Pitbull's music a great addition to Zumba?

❷ What kind of music does Pitbull like, and why?

❸ What does his famous saying *"Dale!"* mean?

Research Project:

❶ What does Pitbull's New Year's Eve special have in common with other New Year's Eve television specials around the world? Find out what kinds of New Year's celebrations people in other countries have. How do they bring in the New Year?

Words to Understand

emigrant: a person who moves from their country to a new country.

oncology: the study of cancer.

linguistic: of or belonging to language.

correlate: to establish a connection.

Chapter 5

Pitbull Delivers a SLAM Dunk in Giving Back to His Community

Growing Up

Before his transformation to international superstar, Armando Pérez grew up in some of the most troubled neighborhoods in Miami, Florida. His parents were **emigrants** from Cuba. Alysha Acosta, his mother, was sent to America as part of Operation Peter Pan in the 1960s. Pitbull's father, José Antonio Armando Pérez Torres, fled Cuba for the United States a few years later.

His parents separated when Pitbull was a toddler. He learned English from children's shows, like *Sesame Street*, while his mother worked. The family's stability was provided by his aunt and grandmother, as he and his mother moved every three to six months to different neighborhoods around Miami as Alysha looked for work.

Tough Miami Spaces

The majority of these areas were overrun by gangs and drugs, and many of the kids growing up there did not think there was any way out of that lifestyle. Pitbull's own father was caught up in the darker side of life in the streets of Miami, illegally making and then losing a fortune during the 1980s.

At sixteen, Pitbull found his way into the drug world of Miami's streets. When his mother found out what he was doing, she kicked him out of her house. This form of discipline is called "tough love"—genuinely concerned parents institute clear consequences for undesirable behavior, and then guide a teen to make the right choice or face the consequences. In Pitbull's case, afterward, he lived alone in some of Miami's worst neighborhoods.

From his present position of international stardom, Pitbull does not talk much about that time in his life. He does not want to glamorize the dangerous life he led as a teenager. He left that lifestyle when he witnessed firsthand the effects drugs have on users. Now he sees that his mother's version of tough love contributed to the man he is today.

Words Are Powerful

Pitbull's early life may have been erratic, but one thing he learned early was the power of words. His father, Armando, required him to memorize the poetry of José Martí, a famous Cuban poet, and from the young age of five, he recited the poems for a crowd. This was the beginning of Pitbull's fascination with the way words can influence people's emotions.

During his school years, his eleventh-grade drama teacher, Hope Martinez, recognized his talent with words and encouraged him to take his **linguistic** gifts farther.

José Martí (1853–1895) —José Martí was a famous Cuban writer involved in efforts to liberate his country from Spanish rule. His criticism of the Spanish government resulted in his arrest and deportation to Spain. While in Spain, he wrote about his terrible treatment during his sentence of hard labor in a Cuban prison. Martí studied law during this time as well.

Martí married Carmen Zayas Bazan, and they returned to Cuba in 1878. They had a son José while living there, but Martí was once again arrested and forced to flee the country.

In 1892, he helped create the Cuban Revolutionary Party, which began to plan to take Cuba back from Spain. The fight began on April 11, 1895, and Martí was killed in battle on May 19. Martí's writings have motivated revolutionary movements around the world.

José Martí, shown on a 1986 Cuban one peso note, was a Cuban national hero—who fought against the Spanish and later the United States, —as well as an important figure in Latin American literature

Becoming Pitbull

Pitbull's high school experience was not ideal, and in his opinion, he was given a diploma at the end of his time at Coral Park High School mainly because the principal did not want him returning for another year. His educational encounters may not have been the best, but his ability to use words to create electrifying lyrics continued to grow.

The name he gave himself, "Pitbull," refers to the struggles he faced during his early life. Pit bull dogs are known for not giving up, and that is how he sees his rise to fame. He did not give up because he came from a poor neighborhood. And he did not give up when trying to move his career forward.

Supporting Miami's Children

The self-proclaimed Mr. 305—referring to the Miami area code—is proud of his heritage, saying, "If you don't know where you're from, you don't know where you're going." It is that ideal that led him to help create SLAM, the Sports Leadership and Management Academy.

This public charter school in the Little Havana neighborhood of Miami opened in 2013, and as of 2016, it has educated 1,000 students in grades six through twelve. Through the integration of Common Core Standards and sports-related themes, SLAM prepares students for careers in the professional sports industry—but not as players. Behind-the-scenes occupations are more stable than playing a sport. This type of charter school was designed to be interesting to students who are bored by traditional public school.

Mater Academy Inc.

SLAM is a part of the Mater Academy network of charter schools. The company has deep Cuban roots that made it a perfect match for Pitbull. The network evolved from Centro Mater, a charitable childcare organization founded in 1968 by Mother Margarita Miranda, a member of the Society of the Sacred Heart in Cuba. The original Centro Mater was built in one of Miami's poorest neighborhoods to care for the needs of the children living there.

Mother Miranda's vision inspired Mater Academy Inc., a non-profit educational organization operating excellent tuition-free charter schools in South Florida. The first school opened in 1998, and in 2010, there were fourteen schools in the network. Sixty-three hundred pre-K through twelfth grade students in Miami-Dade County attended at that time. The number of students rose to over 13,000 by 2015, with schools spanning South Florida. As of 2017, Mater Academy Inc. consists of twenty-six Florida charter schools for students of all backgrounds.

Like Pitbull, they believe every child can do well and must be given the opportunity to do so, because every child matters.

SLAM
SLAM's Intentions

Pitbull is determined to give back to his community, especially Little Havana, through his involvement in the Sports Leadership and Management Academy. He grew up in a low-income family, and the Mater Academy charter schools network is committed to helping students like him. They want to educate the children—and work with their families, as well—to create the first generation of Little Havana college graduates.

The mission statement of SLAM **correlates** with the values Pitbull learned from organized physical activities. The school strives to provide an "innovative and in-depth" program through an emphasis on sports-related majors.

SLAM'S Benefits

Pitbull loved basketball as a kid and says that athletic competition demonstrates a player's discipline. Through sports, students learn that the harder they work, the better they get. The value of a team is also taught through sporting events and while training.

Students at SLAM can focus on sports medicine, business, marketing, health and communication, digital television and sports media production, sport marketing, and entertainment and management. Contrary to the claims of some critics, SLAM does not teach students to be professional athletes. Instead, it guides them through learning about the business around and behind the professional athletics industry. Students experience real-world learning situations in all aspects of various national sports franchises.

SLAM partners with local and national franchises to provide pupils with career mentors and executive internships they would not have access to otherwise. Students are given every opportunity to succeed, and Pitbull feels they should focus on their education because "…nothing is owed to you in life, those who make it work hard for it." He brought SLAM students with him to the 2016 iHeart

Fiesta Latina Awards. They stood with him onstage as he gave an emotional acceptance speech for the Corazon Latino Award.

Pitbull Supports SLAM

This project is so important to Pitbull that he was driven to contribute $15 million of his own money to finance the construction of the SLAM facility. He says he understands the kids who attend SLAM because he lived in many of the neighborhoods they come from, especially Little Havana. The charter school is a way to reach students at a young age and "mold their minds, teach them what it is to be motivated and self-inspired."

Pitbull states in interviews that these students need to learn to believe in themselves because, "coming from the neighborhood we came from no one believed in us … This is changing the world little by little." He is very vocal about his praise of SLAM's students because he sees himself in each one of them.

Other Charitable Activities

Creating and supporting SLAM is not the only way Pitbull gives back to his community.

Together for the Children, the Campaign for Miami's Children

As a celebrity ambassador for Together for the Children, Pitbull helps raise awareness of the Nicklaus Children's Hospital. In 2011, he was part of a "Get Well Soon" tour and visited the hospital's **oncology** unit.

Miami Children's Health Foundation

In 2015, Pérez was inducted into the Ambassador David M. Walters International Pediatric Hall of Fame for his generosity in giving to

Watch the multi-artist video for *Somos El Mundo*

this charity. The hall of fame was created to spotlight individuals who have made large contributions to the health and well-being of children.

Generous Contributor

As discussed, Mr. Worldwide did not grow up in a world of wealth and glamour. His childhood and teenage years were spent living in Miami's poorer neighborhoods. But his determination and continuing hard work have provided the wealth and glamour his childhood lacked. He is dedicated to giving back to the children who are growing up in those same neighborhoods today.

Through his continued support, SLAM is educating students who may otherwise become dropouts. And the patients at Nicklaus Children's Hospital and other children living in Miami are benefiting from his generous donations as well.

Earthquake in Haiti

In 2010, a very large earthquake struck Haiti, an island nation in the Caribbean. It is estimated that almost 100,000 people were killed by the catastrophic quake, and almost 300,000 buildings were destroyed.

Since Haiti is the poorest country in the Western Hemisphere, aid was desperately needed for food, water, and fuel. Haiti's needs have continued to be significant even years after the quake. Pitbull, along with a huge number of Spanish artists, released a charity single called *Somos El Mundo*—an updated Spanish version of the 1985 hit song *We Are the World*. All proceeds from sales of the single were donated to earthquake relief efforts.

Fast Fact 8:

What Is a Charter School?—The first charter school opened in the United States in 1992 in Minnesota. Public charter schools are open to all children, do not charge tuition, and do not have special entrance requirements. Depending on the state law, charter schools can be started by parents, teachers, non-profit groups, or even government agencies. However, charter schools cannot be created without permission from the school district, city, or state in which they plan to operate.

Charter school curriculums are often built with students who need alternative learning methods in mind. They may require more hands-on instruction, or may be attracted to a specialized curriculum.

Pitbull and Charter Schools

SLAM, the charter school Pitbull helped create in Little Havana, is built around the theme of sports management. Other charter schools focus on performing arts, or even college and career preparation. This type of school is able to adjust the curriculum to meet students' needs because the teachers have more influence over the curriculum they teach.

In 2016, there were around 7,000 charter schools in the United States serving around 3 million students. In fact, not only does Pitbull support SLAM, three of his own six children attend charter schools!

Text-Dependent Questions:

❶ What does SLAM stand for?
❷ What kinds of jobs does SLAM prepare students for?
❸ How much of his own money did Pitbull donate to SLAM?

Research Project:

❶ Pitbull's mother left Cuba as part of Operation Peter Pan. Search for more information on Operation Peter Pan, also known as Operación Pedro Pan. Why were children taken out of the country without their parents? Where did they live in the United States?

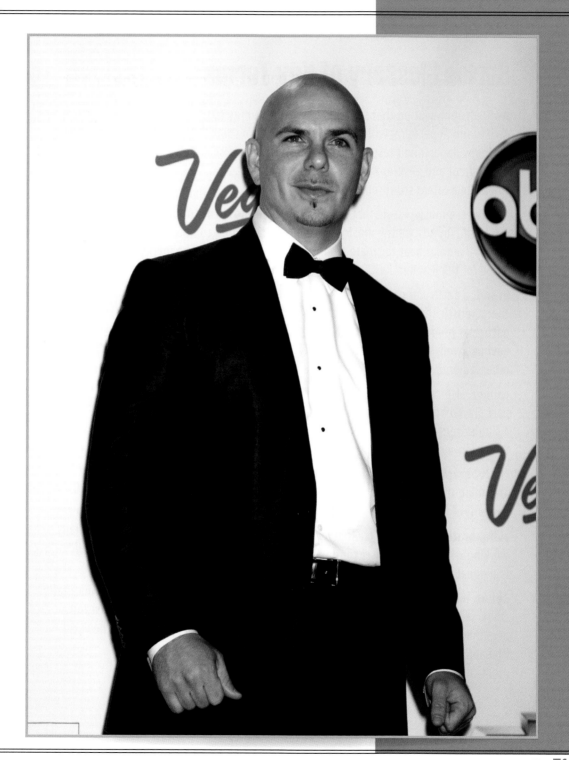

Series Glossary of Key Terms

A&R: an abbreviation that stands for Artists and Repertoire, which is a record company department responsible for the recruitment and development of talent; similar to a talent scout for sports.

ambient: a musical style that relies on electronic sounds, gentle music, and the lack of a regular beat to create a relaxed mood for the listener.

brand: a particular product or a characteristic that serves to identify a particular product; a brand name is one having a well-known and usually highly regarded or marketable word or phrase.

cameo: also called a cameo role; a minor part played by a prominent performer in a single scene of a motion picture or a television show.

choreography: the art of planning and arranging the movements, steps, and patterns of dancers.

collaboration: a product created by working with someone else; combining individual talents.

debut: a first public appearance on a stage, on television, or so on, or the beginning of a profession or career; the first appearance of something, like a new product.

deejay (DJ): a slang term for a person who spins vinyl records on a turntable; aka a disc jockey.

demo: a recording of a new song, or of one performed by an unknown singer or group, distributed to disc jockeys, recording companies, and the like, to demonstrate the merits of the song or performer.

dubbed: something that is named or given a new name or title; in movies, when the actors' voices have been replaced with those of different performers speaking another language; in music, transfer or copying of previously recorded audio material from one medium to another.

endorsement: money earned from a product recommendation, typically by a celebrity, athlete, or other public figure.

entrepreneur: a person who organizes and manages any enterprise, especially a business, usually with considerable initiative and at financial risk.

falsetto: a man singing in an unnaturally high voice, accomplished by creating a vibration at the very edge of the vocal chords.

genre: a subgroup or category within a classification, typically associated with works of art, such as music or literature.

hone, honing: sharpening or refining a set of skills necessary to achieve success or perform a specific task.

icon: a symbol that represents something, such as a team, a religious person, a location, or an idea.

innovation: the introduction of something new or different; a brand-new feature or upgrade to an existing idea, method, or item.

instrumental: serving as a crucial means, agent, or tool; of, relating to, or done with an instrument or tool.

jingle: a short verse, tune, or slogan used in advertising to make a product easily remembered.

mogul: someone considered to be very important, powerful, and in charge; a term usually associated with heads of businesses in the television, movie studio, or recording industries.

performing arts: skills that require public performance, as acting, singing, or dancing.

philanthropy: goodwill to fellow members of the human race; an active effort to promote human welfare.

public relations: the activity or job of providing information about a particular person or organization to the public so that people will regard that person or organization in a favorable way.

sampler: a digital or electronic musical instrument, related to a synthesizer, that uses samples, or sound recordings, of real instruments (trumpet, violin, piano, etc.) mixed with excerpts of recorded songs and other interesting sounds (sirens, ocean waves, construction noises, car horns, etc.) that are stored digitally and can be replayed by a triggering device, like a sequencer, electronic drums, or a MIDI keyboard.

single: a music recording having two or more tracks that is shorter than an album, EP, or LP; also, a song that is particularly popular, independent of other songs on the same album or by the same artist.

Further Reading

Rogers, Ray. *"Pitbull on His Rough Past and His Future as the Next Dick Clark."* OceanDrive, October 27, 2014. https://oceandrive.com/interview-pitbull-opens-up-about-rough-past-family-life-and-new-years-eve-special.

Saddleback Educational Publishing. *Pitbull (Hip-Hop Biographies)*. Saddleback Educational Publishing, Inc., 2013.

Internet Resources

www.billboard.com
The official site of Billboard Music.

www.billboard.biz
Online extension of *Billboard* Magazine.

www.hiphopwired.com
A popular blog for hip-hop fans.

www.hiphopweekly.com
A young adult hip-hop magazine.

www.vibe.com
An American entertainment magazine focusing on R&B and hip-hop artists.

Educational Videos

Chapter 1:
http://x-qr.net/1GBu
http://x-qr.net/1GGV
http://x-qr.net/1F4K
http://x-qr.net/1EaJ
http://x-qr.net/1DK6
http://x-qr.net/1H20
http://x-qr.net/1H7D
http://x-qr.net/1GR5
http://x-qr.net/1Fjq

Chapter 3:
http://x-qr.net/1Gvi
http://x-qr.net/1FHi
http://x-qr.net/1Dfr
http://x-qr.net/1Gbv

Chapter 4:
http://x-qr.net/1HLN

Chapter 5:
http://x-qr.net/1F74

Citations

"It's great to see a kid…" by Luther Campbell. Campbell, Luther. "I Brought up Pitbull from a Pitpuppy." *Miami New Times*, February 17, 2011.

Castillo, Arielle. "Lil Jon Talks Crunk Rock, Pitbull, and fine wine." *Miami New Times*. September 24, 2009.

"I always believed in this guy…" by Lil Jon. Castillo, "Lil Jon Talks…" 2009.

"Rebelution stands for fighter…" by Pitbull. Concepcion, Mariel. "Pitbull Ready for a 'Rebelution.'" *Billboard*, August 14, 2009.

"The world 'revolution' is…" by Pitbull. Concepcion, "Pitbull Ready…" 2009.

"…the best known and influential…" by Leila Cobo, Billboard reporter. "Celia Cruz." Wikipedia, Wikimedia Foundation. Accessed October 09, 2017. https://en.wikipedia.org/wiki/Celia_Cruz.

"Tireless devotion to his community…" by Anitere Flores, President of Doral College. Molloy, Antonia. "Pitbull Given Honorary Degree: A Surprising Achievement for the Rapper." *The Independent*. June 20, 2014.

"…wants [his] kids to excel…" by Pitbull. Muñoz, Jonathan. "Pitbull Describes Endorsement Empire and Road to Stardom in 'Nightline' Interview (VIDEO). *The Huffington Post*. July 31, 2013.

"The world is fascinated by Pitbull's story…" by Ana Martinez, Producer of the Walk of Fame Ceremonies. Barker, Andrew. "Pitbull Receives a Star on the Hollywood Walk of Fame." *Variety*. July 15, 2016.

"I love the hustle…" by Pitbull. Privitera, Alexandra. "Superstar: Only 10% Talent Got Me Here." CNBC. October 20, 2015.

"…hip, innovative, and relevant…" Francois, Olivier. "Dodge Dart Goes Hip with New Commercial Starring Pitbull." Autoevolution.com. July 11, 2013.

"What's better than Mr. 305…" by Pitbull. Walker, Elaine. "Pitbull takes ownership in The New Miami Subs Grill." *Miami Herald*. July 24, 2012.

"Even if you wanted to…" by Pitbull. "24 Crazy Hours with Mr. Worldwide." Interview with Cecilia Vega and ABC News. July 29, 2013.

"Combining Pitbull's already massive…" by Cris Abrego. Littleton, Cynthia. "Pitbull Inks Development Pact with Endemol North America." Interview with Variety.com. January 27, 2014.

"The music business…" by Pitbull. Privitera, "Superstar: Only…" 2015.

"Major names in music…" by Beto Perez. Aguila, Justino. "Lil Jon Joins Zumba Fitness With Single, Upcoming Nightclub Series." *Billboard*. February 20, 2013.

"Zumba is the only…" by Alberto Perlman. Zumba Fitness. "Global Fitness Company, Zumba Fitness, Joins Pitbull on the Euphoria Tour." *PR Newswire*. October 21, 2011.

"The way Zumba has done…" by Pitbull. Markman, Rob. "Pitbull and Wyclef Get Fit with Zumba." *MTV News*. July 15, 2011.

"…defied all the odds…" Estrin, Joshua. "Paulina Rubio, Daddy Yankee and Vanilla Ice Turn Up the Volume on Health and Fitness." *The Huffington Post*. August 22, 2012.

"I just want to make global…" by Pitbull. Robinson, Lisa. "How Pitbull Went from Miami Street Rapper to Global Brand Ambassador." *Vanity*. July 11, 2016.

"With everything that's going on…" by Pitbull. Fox News. "Pitbull Advises to 'Buckle Up' as He Plans Going Full Throttle in the New Year." FoxNews.com. December 27, 2013.

"There's no magic trick…" by Pitbull. Barker, "Pitbull Receives a Star…" 2016.

"If you don't know where…" by Pitbull. Flores, Adolfo. "Pitbull Recounts How His Family's Immigrant Story Gave Him His Own American Dream." *BuzzFeed News*. June 30, 2015.

"…innovative and in-depth…" SLAM mission statement. Accessed October 11, 2017. http://www.slammiami.com/apps/pages/index.jsp?uREC_ID=198960&type=d.

"…nothing is owed to you in life…" by Pitbull. Rogers, Ray. "Pitbull on His Rough Past and His Future as the Next Dick Clark." *OceanDrive*. October 27, 2014.

"…coming from the neighborhood…" by Pitbull. Rogers, "Pitbull on His…" 2014.

Photo Credits

Index

A

Acosta, Alysha, 21–22, 45–46, 61
Advertising techniques, 40–41
Afrojack, 14
Alba, Barbara, 28
Albums
    Armondo, 13
    Boatlift, 12
    Climate Change, 15, 52
    Dale, 15
    El Mariel, 11–12
    Global Warming, 14, 17
    Global Warming: Meltdown, 14
    Globalization, 15
    M.I.A.M.I. (Money Is A Major Issue),
    9, 10–11, 27–28, 51
    Money Is Still A Major Issue, 11
    Pitbull Starring in Rebelution, 12–13
    Planet Pit, 14, 54
American Latin Music Awards, 55
American Latino Media Arts Award, 32
American Music Awards, 32
Awards, 13, 14, 15, 32–33, 55, 67

B

Barker, Travis, 52
Billboard Latin Music Awards, 14, 32
Billboard Music Awards, 13, 14, 33
Birthplace, 21
Broadcast Music Inc. Awards (BMI), 33
Brown, Chris, 52
Buffet, Warren, 46–47
Business ventures, 42–44, 53–56

C

Campbell, Luther, 7–8, 11, 34
Castro, Fidel, 21, 22
Charitable activities, 64–69
Charter school, Pitbull's sponsorship of,
64–67, 69–70
Collaborations
    Afrojack, 14
    Barker, Travis, 52
    Brown, Chris, 52
    Eastside Boyz, 51
    Elephant Man, 11, 51
    Flo Rida, 52
    Iglesias, Enrique, 15, 51, 52
    Ke$ha, 52
    Kelly, R., 15
    Lil Jon, 51
    Lopez, Jennifer, 14, 15, 52–53
    LunchMoney Lewis, 52
    Perry, Joe, 52
    Pretty Ricky, 51
    Shakira, 14
    Thicke, Robin, 15, 52
    Usher, 51
    Ying Yang Twins, 11, 51
Crunk-style music, 8, 10
Cruz, Celia, 26, 34
Cuban cultural influence, 11–12, 23–25

D

Diaz Brothers Management, 8
Dr. Pepper endorsement, 37

Index

E

Eastside Boyz, 51
Education, importance of, 28, 64–67
Elephant Man, 11, 51
Endemol Shine North America, 43–44, 56–57
Endorsements, 34–42
Enrique Iglesias and Pitbull Live tour, 17–18
E!'s Inside Track Summer Concert Series, 17
Euphoria Tour, 54

F

Family members, 21–22, 28, 61
Fiat Chrysler Automobiles endorsement, 38–39
FIFA World Cup Anthem, 53
Flo Rida, 17, 52
Fragrance Lines by Pitbull, 44

G

Grammy Awards, 15, 33

H

Haiti earthquake relief, 68–69
Hip-hop music
crunk style, 8
Miami bass genre of, 26
Hollywood Walk of Fame star, 34
Honey I'm Home production company, 56–57

I

Iglesias, Enrique, 15, 17–18, 51, 52, 54

iHeart Fiesta Latina Awards, 66–67
Interviews
    ABC News, 42
    Billboard Magazine, 16
    CNBC, 45
    Miami New Times, 9
    MTV News, 55
    Variety magazine, 57, 58

K

Ke$ha, 17, 52
Kelly, R., 15
Kodak endorsement, 37

L

Latin Grammy Awards, 33
Leitte, Claudia, 53
Lil Jon, 8–9, 11, 51
Lo Nuestro Award, 13, 33
Lopez, Jennifer, 14, 15, 52–53
Luke Records, 7
LunchMoney Lewis, 52

M

Mariel boatlift, 12, 22
Martí, José, 23, 62–63
Martinez, Hope, 62
Mater Academy, Inc., 65
Men in Black 3 movie theme song, 14
Mentors, 45–48
Miami, drug trade in, 23, 27, 61–62
Miami Children's Health Foundation, 67–68
Miami Subs Grill endorsement, 41–42
Miranda, Mother Margarita, 65

Index

MP3 Music Awards, 13
Mr. 305. see Pitbull
Mr. Worldwide. see Pitbull

N
Nas, 25
New Year's Eve Special, 56–57
North American Tour, 17
Norwegian Cruise Line
endorsement, 38

O
Operation Peter Pan, 61
OutKast, 11

P
Pérez, Armando. see Pitbull
Perez, Beto, 54–55
Perry, Joe, 52
Pitbull
    birthplace, 21
    as a brand name, 53–56
    catchphrase, 58
    childhood of, 27, 61–64
    Cuban heritage of, 11–12, 23–25
    family of, 12, 21–22, 28, 61
Planet Pit Tour, 16–17
Pretty Ricky, 51

R
Rap
    Dirty South style of, 10
    freestyle, 7
    Southern style of, 7
    West Coast style of, 26

Rebelution Tour, 16
Robbins, Tony, 45–46
Role models, musical, 25–26

S
Shakira, 14
Sirius XM Radio Station, 43
Slim, Carlos, 48
Social media presence, 36–37
Sports Leadership and Management
Academy, 64–67, 69–70

T
Thicke, Robin, 15, 52
Together for the Children, 67
Torres, José Armando Pérez, 12, 23,
61–62
Tours, 16–18, 54
Trick Daddy, 11

U
Usher, 51

Y
Ying Yang Twins, 11, 51

Z
Zumba Fitness partnership, 53–56

Author's Biography

Summer Bookout is a freelance writer who works on a variety of projects for many different clients. She has a master's degree in English literature from Mercy College. Her favorite hobby is reading, and she loves to spend time with her two children.